Preventing Weapon Crime and Gang Membership

A Toolkit for those working with Young People

Angelique Flemming

authorHOUSE®

AuthorHouse™ UK Ltd.
500 Avebury Boulevard
Central Milton Keynes, MK9 2BE
www.authorhouse.co.uk
Phone: 08001974150

Published by AuthorHouse   4/30/2012

ISBN: 978-1-4520-4021-9 (sc)

This book is printed on acid-free paper.

Background to this book

This resource draws evidence from many official sources such as British Crime Surveys, Offending, Crime and Justice Surveys and Youth Justice Surveys commissioned by the Youth Justice Board and carried out by Ipsos MORI.

The suggested activities within this book are based on the Home Office's national initiative, TKAP (Tackling Knives Action Programme) that was rolled out in 2009.

This national initiative directed local services to tackle weapon carrying and knife crime incidents by placing a focus on the following areas:

Attitudes to knife crime
Peer education
Social implications
Health and medical implications
First Aid and public space awareness
Managing conflict
The law
Victim Awareness

This book is aimed at those working with children and young people and acts as a supportive resource and toolkit which can be used to engage young people in understanding the risks and consequences of weapon crime and gang affiliation. This journey of learning should allow young people to become fully informed with regards to decision making and positive group membership.

Suggested activities throughout this resource are based around the key areas mentioned above. Although these activities are encouraged, they are not prescriptive. Therefore, as a professional working with young people, you should pitch activities suited to learner needs, such as age, ability and preferred learning style.

Preface

This toolkit was developed by a lead author of the Liverpool Youth Offending Service (YOS) Knife Possession Prevention Programme (KPPP).

An overwhelming positive formal review and evaluation of the KPPP, undertaken by the Home Office led to the authour, Angelique Flemming, receiving an award in 2009 from the Criminal Justice Service for 'outstanding contribution towards tackling knife crime'.

This award led the authour to believe that through an educative approach, young people could become empowered to make independent decisions in relation to weapon carrying. The ranges of activities provided throughout this toolkit are aimed at achieving this outcome and may be used with any age group.

Information and guidance is provided throughout this book to allow those using the toolkit to become familiar with the background knowledge needed to enhance understanding of weapon related crime and gang membership.

PAL

Using this Toolkit

The overall aims and learning outcomes for young people taking part in weapon carrying, crime and gang membership awareness lessons are;

For young people to clearly understand what is classed as an 'offensive' weapon by being given the opportunity to receive and relay legislative information

For young people to positively support peer learning and influence through group debate, discussion and reflection, around the management of conflict and prevention of reprisal

For young people to become fully informed about the physical, criminal and social consequences associated with weapon crime by studying public, media and societal views

For young people to demonstrate understanding of the physical, emotional, financial and psychological impact for victims of weapon crime by studying, reviewing and concluding case study material

For young people to become informed about the formation of 'gangs' and the associated risks and consequences attached to gang membership, by studying the characteristics and criminal operations of 'gangs'

For young people to have the opportunity to use their peer dialogue within a safe environment to find alternative, safe strategies, which will hopefully allow all students to feel safe that weapon carrying amongst their own peer group has been agreed as wrong, dangerous and forbidden

Contents

PAL

- Peer Group Agreement
- Discussion Points / Cards
- Art Work
- If I ruled the World for 1 Day!
- M'Lord
- Media Headlines

Weapon carrying – what's it all about?

Weapon carrying is not a new phenomenon. What is new, are the areas of criminality relating to the carrying of weapons and the age of those carriers increasingly falling within the young person population.

Knife carrying is the most common form of knife related offences but it creates no specifically recorded harmed victims until the knife is actually used to inflict injury. [1]

UK Firearms, Knife and Weapon laws have evolved over the past 50 years. Chronologically, these laws are;

The Prevention of Crime Act (1953)

Law - It became an offence to have an offensive weapon in a public place: including any article made or adapted for use for causing injury to any person.

Penalty - Up to 4 years imprisonment and/ or fine

The Restrictions of Offensive Weapons Act (1959)

Law - The manufacture, sale, purchase, hire or lending of Flick knives and Gravity knives became banned.

Penalty - Up to 6 months imprisonment and / or fine up to £5000.

---

1   'Knife Crime', a review of Evidence and Policy: 2nd Ed: Centre for Crime and Justice Studies, p11

PAL

The Criminal Justice Act (1988)

Law - Published a list of prohibited Martial Arts style weapons. It became an offence to carry an article with a blade or sharp point in a public place.

Penalty - Up to 6 months imprisonment and / or fine up to £5000.

The Public Order Act (1994)

Contains a power under which a Police Officer of Inspector rank or above can authorise Police officers, within a given area, to stop and search for offensive weapons or dangerous instruments for up to 24 hours.

The Offensive Weapons Act (1996)

Law - Prohibited the sale of knives to under 16 year olds.

Penalty - Up to 6 months imprisonment and / or fine up to £5000

The Knives Act (1997)

Law - Prohibits the sale of Combat knives.

Penalty - Up to 2 years imprisonment and / or fine.

Violent Crime Reduction Act (2006)

Law – This Act introduced the following restrictions;

Banned the sale of knives to anyone under 16 years of age

Raised the minimum age (up from 16 to 18 years of age) at which a young person could buy a knife/bladed article.

Introduced powers for School Heads and teachers to search pupils for knives

Reduced the threshold for a Police Constable to enter the school grounds and search suspected knife carriers

Created a new offence of using another person to mind or secure a weapon

Created an aggravated offence where the offence involves a child or young person

Generally speaking, knives where the blade folds into the handle (Swiss Army Penknife) are not illegal. However, the blade length had to be less than 3inches, if being carried in public. Also, if this small blade is used to threaten or harm someone else then that possession becomes illegal rather than legal.

The law now clearly states that any person;

Carrying an article with a blade or sharp point in a public place without good reason shall face a fine up to £5000 or a custodial sentence of up to 4 years

In recent years there has been a significant rise in weapon related crime amongst teenagers. It is an ever-evolving area of study that poses many questions for professionals attempting to eradicate fear from communities and alter attitudes towards carrying and using weapons.

These questions are:

Why do young people feel the need to arm themselves with a weapon?

Why do young people become entrenched in gang membership?

Who are young people influenced by?

What are the barriers to social inclusion for some young people?

What are the consequences of social exclusion?

Is weapon carrying amongst young people a myth or are the media right?

Some of the reasons for young people carrying weapons are listed below;

Territorial conflict
Protection
Sense of belonging
Status
Fear
Safety
Fashion
Revenge
Peer pressure/ influence
Financial/material gain from crime
Social exclusion
Societal exclusion
Drugs/Alcohol influences
Lack of aspiration/motivation/attainment
Boredom
Respect
'Buzz'
Poor anger management
Male image
Lack of communication skills
'No Grass' mentality

A report by the Bridge House Trust, *Fear and Fashion,* which gained the views of practitioners working with young people, concluded that *'fear of crime, experience of victimisation* (either directly or indirectly) *and the desire for status in an unequal society are key motivators for young people to carry knives and weapons'.* [2]

It should be highlighted to the students that there are very clear messages given by the British legislative system – that a weapon will never be legally classed as a '**defensive**' weapon but will always be classed as an '**offensive**' weapon, even where the carrier/attacker was under pressure to 'protect' themselves. This is due to the fact that the law clearly states that it is against

---

2   Lemos, G. 2004, Fear and Fashion: The use of Guns and Knives and other weapons by young people, London: Lemos & Carne, p8-11

the law to be in possession of a weapon in a public place, therefore leaving no legally defensible excuse for the carrying or use of that weapon.

Figures provided by the Home Office 2005 Offending, Crime and Justice survey of 10-25 year olds, revealed that of the 4% who had disclosed they had carried a knife, those types of knives were;

Penknife 41%
Flick Knife 29%
Other Knives 20%
Kitchen Knife 10% [3]

3   Wilson, D. Sharp, C. And Patterson, A. (2006), Young People and Crime: Findings from the 2005 Offending, Crime and Justice Survey, London: Home Office, p27

PAL

Current Preventative Strategies

National Knife Amnesty

According to the Home Office, a total of 89,864 knives were handed in during the 2005 – 2006 British knife amnesties.[4]

Stop and Search

Under Section 60 of the Public Order Act 1994, between 2001 and 2002, 1367 people were found to be carrying an offensive weapon or dangerous instrument.[5]

Increased Prison sentences

The *Violent Crime Reduction Act 2006* saw the government raise the maximum prison term for carrying a knife in a public place without lawful reason, up from 2 years to 4 years.

Increased search rights for teaching Personnel

Under the Violent Crime Reduction Act 2006, all staff in school now have the power to search students to look for knives or offensive weapons. This search does not immediately

---

4   [4] Knives off our streets make our communities safer, Home Office Press Release 097/2006, July 2006

5   Brookman, F. & Maguire, M. (2003), reducing Homicide: A review of the possibilities, Home Office Online Report, 20001 -200 03, p33-34

require the presence of police, therefore providing a quick response to suspected weapon carrying in schools.

Education

The Government has ploughed millions of pounds into programmes which offer creative, educative alternatives to the traditional, punitive response to knife related crime.

These programmes of work have been mainly targeted at disaffected, marginalised young people, whom are engaged with statutory criminal justice services, and excluded from mainstream involvement.

What is an 'Offensive' weapon?

As a starting point, ask the young people what they would consider to be an 'offensive' weapon. This exercise could be as an open discussion or as an activity. Have students produce a list of their ideas and then discuss the overall definition of an 'offensive' weapon. To help students it may be worthwhile giving them this definition as defined within the *Prevention of Crime Act 1953;*

An Offensive Weapon is;

'any article made or adapted for use for causing injury to the person, or intended by the person having it with him for such use by him or some other person'.

The feedback provided from the students should be similar to the list of 'offensive' weapons detailed below;

Guns
Knives
Saw
Glass bottle
Axe

Sports bats
Sword
Knuckle Dusters
Stanley blades
Laser pens
Kitchen knife
Screw Driver
Fishing Knife
Scissors
Hammer
Snooker Cue
Pen

As defined, an offensive weapon is 'anything intended to cause harm'. Therefore, encourage the students to consider the whole range of items, which could be used as a weapon and classed as offensive.

N.B. The only Guns legalised in England are Shotguns and Rifles, mainly for the purposes of hunting sports. These Guns have to kept in a locked enclosure by law. Assault Rifles are banned.

Legalised Gun owners are required by law to have a fully legitimate licence. Laws and offences relating to the possession and use of Guns come under the Firearms Act. Possession of a Firearm carries a 5-year jail term.

The sale of, and possession of, a replica / imitation Firearm is also illegal.

Workshop suggestion

Ask the students to consider which of the items listed as being 'offensive' weapons are legal and which are illegal to make, sell or be in possession of. Students could also rank the danger of each offensive weapon.

This should generate some interesting debate and discussion and provide you, the tutor, with an understanding of the student's perceptions of weapon crime.

End this phase by asking students to consider how easy it is, particularly for young people to gain access to these weapons. Feedback should evidence

that it is much easier for young people to gain a bladed or offensive weapon rather than a gun. This may suggest an explanation as to why knife crime is prominent within the adolescent generation compared with gun crime.

Attitudes and Perceptions

Young people's attitudes and perceptions related to weapon carrying should now be explored.

This will allow you to offer young people a non judgemental tone to the lessons. The key message is to allow young people to feel safe to talk openly and honestly about their feelings towards weapon carrying.

Both young people who do, and do not, carry weapons should feel they have a worthwhile contribution to make towards this learning cycle, rather than feel already pre-judged to be a weapon carrier.

You could have the students design an attitudinal questionnaire, which asks some pertinent questions of the young people, such as;

> Do a lot of young people just say they are carrying a weapon, to make themselves sound threatening?

> Is weapon carrying amongst young people really a problem in this country?

> Does the media 'hype' up weapon crime?

> Can the excuse of a weapon being used for defensive purposes save you from facing criminal prosecution?

> If you carry a weapon, does it make you feel safer?

> Can a bladed article cause as much damage as a gun?

Is it fair that young people face criminal prosecution for carrying weapons?

Workshop suggestion

Have the young people design their own questionnaire using the Personal Computer (PC), drawing or graphic skills. An anti weapon carrying slogan or logo could be designed and used on the questionnaire.

The young people could use this questionnaire to assess the attitudes of their fellow friends and family, as well as each other's attitudes as class peers.

Comparisons may be drawn between the different groups of questionnaire participants to determine any differences or similarities in attitudes towards weapon carrying. These comparable groups could be based on gender, age and status.

The results of the questionnaire could be quantitatively and qualitatively presented to support an overall conclusion.

Alternatively, this activity could be a simple brainstorming exercise, whereby individual student attitudes are captured onto a questionnaire, Post-It note or Flipchart.

The results of this activity should generate some interesting debate amongst the peers. The results may indicate the extent of weapon carrying amongst the group members.

An overall assessment can be made about the group's attitudes towards weapon carrying. Even if students claim to not have any inclination to carry a weapon, encourage them to still be an active team player and that their positive attitude is what society is relying on to help eradicate weapon related crime.

Ensure all students feel that they have a valuable contribution to make. Young people who are inclined to carry weapons should hopefully

share their fears with the other students and receive some positive peer support.

Dialogue skills amongst young people are imperative if they are to feel safe amongst their peers. Poor communication skills will break down cohesion and escalate conflict, therefore this is a vital opportunity for the young people to air their views and fears within a safe and secure environment.

Physical Consequences

Students should be introduced to the holistic impact of weapon related crime. Physical, Social and Criminal consequences associated with weapon related offending should be introduced, explored and fully understood by the students, from both perspectives of victims and perpetrators.

The following is a basic introduction to the physical consequences associated with weapon use;

Injury - Trauma is described as any body wound or shock produced by a sudden physical accident, injury or attack.

In medical terminology, Blunt Trauma, Blunt injury, Non-penetrating trauma and Blunt force trauma all refer to a type of physical trauma caused to a body part(s) due to impact, injury or physical attack.

These traumas can lead to concussion, abrasion, laceration and bone fracturing. Blunt trauma is contrasted with penetrating trauma, where an object such as a bullet enters the body.

A stabbing is the penetration of a sharp pointed object at close range. Stabbing differs from 'slashing' or 'cutting' in that the motion of the sharp object is moved perpendicular to, and directly into, the victim's body, rather than being drawn across it.

Internal bleeding is just as dangerous as external bleeding. If enough blood vessels are severed to cause serious injury, the skins elasticity will do nothing to prevent blood exiting the circulatory system and accumulating in other parts of the body.

Death from stabbing is caused by shock, severe blood loss, infection or loss of functioning of an essential organ such as the lungs or heart.

Wounds - Incision wounds are often referred to as 'slash' wounds. These are neat, clear-cut, slices to the skin. An incision wound is longer as opposed to deeper. Incision wounds are often found on victim's hands as a result of self defence against a sharp weapon. Lacerations are the thick tearing of the skin, caused by Blunt Trauma. Rough, ragged edges to the wound result. Lacerations cause bruising and abrasion to the edge of the wound and the surrounding tissue. Wounds tend to be deeper as opposed to longer, causing serious damaging contact with tendons, vessels and nerves.

Brain Damage - Different areas of the brain control different human actions and behaviours. Damage to any of these areas can affect mental and physical activity controlled by that part of the brain, as explained below;

Movement, Co-ordination and Balance

> Damage to the brain resulting in movement and mobility difficulties usually happens to the motor cortex, the brain stem and the cerebellum parts of the brain. As one side of the brain affects the motor co-ordination on the opposite side to the body, one can often experience weakness or paralysis of one side.

Dyspraxia

> This is a disorder resulting in deliberate voluntary actions, or sequences of actions. This causes cognition problems and difficulties in being able to put movements together in an orderly, deliberate and intentional way.

Loss of sensation

> Different parts of the sensory cortex deal with sensations in smell, hearing, sight and taste. If the sensory cortex is torn, it is unlikely that part of the brain will function correctly again. Processing what the eyes see is carried out in the Occipital Lobe at the back of the brain. Damage here can result in full or partial blindness, or gaps in the visual field.

Tiredness

Energy stores are quickly depleted if one suffers brain damage, and energy reserves take time to be built up again. This fatigue or exhaustion is attributable to extra physical burden.

Speaking/Swallowing complications

Damage, particularly to the cranial nerve, can result in dysphagia. Muscles for articulation of speech become week and un-coordinated. This condition affects one's ability to swallow and chew, and may cause speech to become slurred and slower. Some people need to be tube fed and have severe speech difficulties.

Bladder/Bowel incontinence

Continence is a cognitive skill as well as a physical skill. Basic skills such as toilet use often have to be re-learned by people affected by brain damage. Other factors affecting continence are medication, physical disability, communication difficulties and sheer embarrassment.

Hormonal changes

Damage to the pituitary gland can occur as a result of brain injury. This pituitary gland controls the body's hormones. Damage to this gland can dramatically impact upon and change a person's hormones, feelings and mood.

Epilepsy

Injury to the brain in the form of a scar increases the risk of an epileptic attack. This is more likely in a penetrating injury – where the skull has been fractured or the brain has been pierced by the skull, or a foreign object, such as a knife. The resulting scar causes the electrical activity in that area of the brain to become unstable and liable to outbursts of uncontrollable activity. A person is not considered free of epileptic seizures until 2 or 3 years of being epileptic free has passed. A driving licence has to be handed in for the period

that a person remains at risk of having an epileptic seizure. Also, certain jobs bar people who pose a risk to themselves or others because of their epileptic condition.

Disability - Many types of disability can result from weapon related injuries. Limbs may be lost in order to save other body parts. Nerve damage may occur or even death. Mobility may be almost impossible due to disability and a victim could become reliant upon a wheelchair. This all adds extra burden and costs to daily functioning.

Scarring - Scarring is guaranteed from any type of weapon related wound. The physical changes in the attackers/victim's body are permanent reminders of the fear, sadness and pain endured. Societal reactions to the survivors changed bodies present the additional trauma of feeling rejected, isolated, unworthy and humiliated. People, who have once been physically 'normal', left disfigured by their injuries, must discover new ways of accommodating body movements to accomplish a once simple task. Constant explanation of scarring has to be given by survivors if their scars are visible to others. Such things as job interviews and relationships become complex and uncomfortable.

Workshop suggestion

Provide students with a variety of newspaper headlines. Some suggested headlines are at the end of this resource, within the 'suggested creative activities' chapter. Current, local headlines can provide a more relative study base for the students. These headlines should be related to weapon crime.

Students should study the headlines and consider the consequential impact upon both the victim and the offender. They should attempt to elaborate on the headline to create a story which depicts the horrific physical, emotional, financial and psychological suffered by the victim.

The headline should be accompanied by a fictional report which describes the headline in great detail. These details could include the age and characteristics of the victim and offender, as well as lifestyle and career habits. The report should almost become a bibliographical and chronological 'story' about the headline.

The 'story' should end on a poignant note, detailing the possible negative consequences for victims, offenders, communities and society, which may have resulted from the real life headline. This should allow students to demonstrate an understanding of the work covered so far.

Gang Membership

'Group' offending is often referred to as 'Gang' membership. The status and characteristics of these 'Gangs' can differ depending on the ultimate purpose of the gang, as explained below.

This area of study shall allow you to raise your levels of understanding of gang culture, enabling you to inform students of the negative aspects of gang membership. Students will be able to differentiate between 'Group' membership and 'Gang' membership by being aware of the behaviours which contribute towards and support gang activity.

For the purposes of keeping the subject of gang membership relative to student experiences, focus should be placed on the study of 'youth' gangs as opposed to organised 'adult' gangs.

Throughout this section students should become informed about;

The differences between 'groups' and 'gangs' of young people.

The types of crimes committed by gang members.

The reasons for young people joining a criminalised gang

The signs of gang operation and existence

The holistic consequences of gang membership upon self, families, communities and society.

PAL

The recruitment strategies adopted by gang members to 'initiate' membership.

The positive and negative aspects of gang membership.

The reasons for young people joining a 'Gang' have been increasingly asked by the public, parents and criminal justice and governmental services.

Often, young people claim that they are simply part of a 'Group' rather than a 'Gang'. This may be so, but there are some distinctions which young people should be informed of which may help to identify a 'Gang' as opposed to a 'Group'.

The definitions offered below provide some guidance for young people;

A 'Gang' is a consistent, re-occurring meeting of young people, mostly based within the streets of their local neighbourhood, who have a gang name and who believe the use of violence is integral to that 'Gangs' identity and status.

A 'Group' is a small, unorganised gathering of young people who choose to occupy the same space and have a common history with one another. Crime and the use of violence are not needed to support the group's identity, existence or status.

An 'Organised Gang' is a group of people consisting of criminalised members whom operate primarily to serve financial gain.

The History of 'Gangs'

Gang membership has evolved throughout the generations. American gangs stretch as far back as the 1800's and the most dated gang culture probably dates back to 'Piracy'. Some well established modern day American gangs are the 'Crips' and the 'Bloods'.

The growth of the British 'Gang Culture' remains an area of emerging research. However, dating back to the World Wars of the 1900's, there is evidence which suggests that 'organised' criminal gangs were in existence and that these gangs were involved in offences for financial gain, such as bank, casino and post office robberies.

Gangs of the 1960 / 1970's were adult led by notorious criminals such as The 'Krays' and 'Mad Frankie Frazer'. Youth culture and Youth groups were still emerging during these eras and from the 1950's onwards, subcultures of the British youth population began to be formed, such as Mods and Teddy Boys, Rockers and Skinheads.

Crime intelligence and forensic evidence became fully embedded into the British criminal justice system during the 1980's. Security initiatives, such as Closed Circuit Television (CCTV) and alarm detectors began to make crimes, such as robbery, much harder to commit without criminals being identified and reprimanded. Also, DNA (DeoxyriboNucleic Acid) evidence began to be a reliable source to prove guilt during the 1980's.

For these reasons, trends in crime committed by gang members began to shift. The 1980's saw the world's illegal drugs trade markets emerge. This became the 'easy' and 'attractive' way to earn cash for criminals and gangs. Once operational drug gangs were in existence, street gangs within large Urban cities were targeted to become the operational, drug selling 'youth' gangs, led by the well organised 'adult' gangs. Weapon related offending associated with the drugs trade then began to become an issue in Britain.

Research by the Youth Justice Board (YJB) identifies 3 types of Youth gangs;

Peer Groups
Street Gangs
Organised Criminal Networks

Society's perceptions and experiences of 'youth' gangs is that they are unruly, disrespectful, delinquent, dangerous and criminal. The Home Office 2004 quoted a delinquent group as;

A group of 3 or more young people

A group who spend a lot of time hanging out in a public place

A group who have existed for 3 months or more

A group who have committed crime together in the last 12 months

A group of young people who claim to have a gang name

A group of young people who claim possession over a particular area

A group of young people who identify a leader

A group of young people who abide by a group code of practice and loyalty

Currently, there are at least 180 gangs in London (Scotland Yard) and at least 170 gangs in Glasgow (Centre for Social Justice). Youth gang members tend to be aged between the ages of 13 and 21 years. Also, gang membership is not exclusive to males, with female lead gangs rising alongside male gangs.

Whilst there is no particular overarching reason for young people becoming entrenched in local gang culture, some of the estimated reasons are;

Peer Pressure - Joining the local 'gang' because their friends do seems a common route into gang membership for youths. Some Teenagers are not confident in assertive dialogue with their peers and may therefore be coerced into gang activity. Young people are known to be fearful of ridicule and alienation from their fellow peers and also of possible physical intimidation and bullying.

Protection - A lot of young people join gangs because other local youth gangs exist and it is viewed as a safety measure to be part of another large, feared gang, rather than face possible conflict or attack when alone. Young people also carry weapons as a safety measure against threat of attack from other gang members.

Familial factors - Some young people may be missing an integral element of a positive childhood experience – positive belonging and self worth. Therefore, gang membership may offer a young person the feeling of belonging to a 'family', where loyalty and teamwork is paramount to gang existence. Young people will often be given specific roles within that gang which will create some self worth and esteem.

Boredom - Young people, who lack a sense of direction and positive use of their leisure time, tend to behave in ways which promote a level of negative excitement and achievement. Poor self esteem may also contribute towards boredom and motivation levels of young people. Some images and messages fed to young people through music, media, video games etc, promote the excitement associated with gang membership, weapon carrying and criminalised behaviours. Young people who are not positively engaged with appropriate activity will be influenced into believing these images are to be aspired to.

Financial/Material gain - Low and poor attainment can mean young people are not academically or educationally equipped or qualified to become motivated into entering a legal career. These young people then become involved in gang membership which can allow for a financial income to be generated through criminal activities. Gang associated crime can appear as an attractive, easy and fast way to gain cash. Gang offending carries a collective effort and responsibility ('no grass' mentality) therefore making gang membership appear as an attractive way to earn money. Young people are part of an ever changing materialistic culture. Capitalist societies are driven by consumerism therefore causing some young people to feel unfairly disadvantaged and envious of the material wealth of others.

Naivety - Some young people become vulnerable to gang recruitment and membership because they lack understanding and knowledge of the associated consequences. Young people may lack positive advisory role models, and therefore become 'parented' by the 'street' and vulnerable to gang affiliation.

PAL

Some other reasons why young people join gangs are;

To feel respected
To gain secure friends
For the feeling of 'power'
To feel a sense of belonging
To feel accepted amongst peers
To defend territory / area
For the 'buzz'

Some of the distinctions, which help to identify a 'gang', are:

The group have an identifiable gang name recognised by its members
Violence is key to the group's identity
Violence promotes solidarity amongst gang members
The gang members claim ownership of identified 'territory' and the gang has a 'leader'
The gang members adopt signs of membership (tattoos, clothing, jewellery, graffiti etc)
Gang members believe in collective group responsibility
Group responsibility reaps group honour

The types of crime committed by 'Gang' members include;

Robbery
Selling stolen goods
Drug offences
Weapon carrying
Weapon selling
'Joyriding'
Graffiti
Criminal damage
Theft

Burglary
Car crime
Assault
Fraud
Racial crime
Anti-Social behaviour

Recruitment of young people may be encouraged or forced by gang members through;

Bullying, pressure and intimidation or threat
Friendship
Bribery to join
The rewarding of drugs/money/material items
Emotional Extortion
'Initiation'
The offering of promise and belonging

The structure of an established 'Gang' normally follows the pattern below. A report commissioned by 'Urban Dynamics' identifies 7 different tiers to gang structure;

Gang Leader - All gangs are characterised by the authoritarian style of management (Klein 2001), therefore that 'leader' determines the level of criminal activity the gang will operate, and this activity reflects the characteristics of the gang leader. This gang leader will have the most power in making day-to-day decisions on behalf of the gang.

Hardcore members - These members tend to be the older ones, whom are culturally and criminally entrenched in gang membership and activity. These members see their role within the gang as one for life. These hardcore members can normally be relied on for violent behaviour and are so entrenched that they find it impossible to exit the gang.

Associate members - These members are committed to the gang's culture and ideologies and aspire to become a hardcore member. Associate members see these hardcore members as role models of how to 'move up' the gang structure.

Clique members - These members, although not entrenched

within the established gang, tend to 'hang' around one or two of the hardcore members. Clique groups may be formed out of fringe, wanna-be and could-be members.

Fringe members - Fringe gang members are just that - on the fringe of full gang membership. These members enter and exit an established gang at free will, and make no long-term commitment to gang membership or loyalty.

Wanna-be members - These are not fully accepted gang members. They are young people who aspire to claiming a place within an established gang, and may even know some gang members. Wanna-be's would commit criminal activities in attempt to impress established gang members and hope of becoming recruited into the gang.

Could-be members - These tend to be young children who have siblings involved in gang membership, or who live in an area closely linked to established gangs. The risk of close gang affiliation is high amongst these groups of children and young people.

The negative risk factors associated with gang affiliation and membership are;

Where gangs are fully operational, local young people become the targets as future 'recruits'

Disjointed family networks can create poor parenting and inconsistent boundary setting within the home

Poor use of recreational and leisure time

Viewing of explicitly violent material/music

Poor self-esteem, motivation and attainment

Poor adult supervision

Lack of communication and assertiveness skills

Exposure to sibling gang members

Glamour of 'easy' money through drugs operations

Lack of ETE status

Irrational decision-making

Rebelliousness against authoritative services

Lack of parental acceptance of a child's gang affiliation or membership

Gangland.net quotes gang membership as falling within 3 tiers of behaviour;

Reputation

> The reputation of the whole gang is of ultimate importance to its members. Individual reputation is also important in determining status or rank of each member within a gangs operation

Respect

> Respect is gained through instilling fear into local youths and community members

Revenge

> Revenge occurs in response to territorial wars or 'disrespect'. Underworld crime on crime creates a revenge mentality

Workshop suggestion

Students should explore the differences between 'Groups' and 'Gangs' of young people. It should be noted that not all groups of young people are identified as a gang. Students could participate in an exercise that explores the characteristics of a 'gang' as opposed to a 'group'. Some discussion points to be raised are;

> What is a gang?
> What is a group?
> What **Gangs** do the students know about?
> What **Groups** do the students know about?
> How new/old is gang culture?
>
> Should all 'youth' groups be classed as gangs for safety of all young people?

Students could search the Internet to identify as many well-known 'Gangs' as they can find and then use this information to produce a news report based on a well-known gang. Comparisons could be drawn between present and past notorious 'Gangs', and well-known gangs from countries such as America.

Students should attempt to demonstrate their understanding of the differences between 'Groups' and 'Gangs' in relation to criminalised behaviour. Plenty of 'Groups' may be identified, such as; Goth's, Rockers, Emo's, Skaters, Bikers, Brownies, Scouts, Football, Chess, Youth Clubs etc. The differences between 'Groups' and 'Gangs' in our present day should be explored so young people may feel informed about whether they themselves are part of a collective 'Group' or a criminalised 'Gang'.

Once students understand gang culture they may begin to explore the pros and cons of gang membership. The benefits for young people joining a gang are as outlined so far. The consequences may be;

> Loss of positive friendships
> Limb loss
> Disability
> Brain Damage
> Paralysis
> Death
> Family death

Probation Orders
Prison sentences
Life of Crime
Community hatred
Family hatred
Gang conflict
Murder
Haunted conscience
Violence
Fines
Criminal record
Lack of employability

Conflict Management

It was reported by Steve Sinnott, General Secretary of the NUT (National Union of Teachers), following an annual conference that;

25% of schools suffer a daily occurrence of violence

22% of Union members had encountered pupils carrying knives

19% of Union members had encountered pupils carrying Drugs [6]

Findings from the 2005 Offending, Crime and Justice Survey revealed that the most commonly reported offence amongst 10-25 year olds was Assault. Similarly the most commonly reported forms of victimisation were Assault. [7]

This 2005 study also commented that the majority of serious offenders had committed, within the last 12 months, an Assault resulting in injury from minor bruising and scratches to serious injuries. Assaults accounted for 44% of all the offences reported by the study participants.

Weapon carrying amongst young people is particularly prominent where dispute has occurred. Young people may feel protected against the threat of attack or injury if they are armed with a weapon.

It is hoped that the students are beginning to understand the implications of weapon related crime, and can make clear connections between weapon carrying and weapon use.

6   Insight Security 2008
7   Wilson D, Sharp C, Patterson A, Young People and Crime: findings from the 2005 Offending, Crime and Justice survey, Home Office P10, 2006

33

Inform students of the unpredictable nature of weapon related conflict. Young people may believe that they are 'protecting' themselves by carrying a weapon, but statistical evidence strongly suggests that a weapon is often turned on the carrier, rather than the target.

Students should reflect on any conclusions they have made about the reasons why young people carry weapons, and begin to consider an ultimate contributing factor to weapon carrying – poor conflict management.

Explain the 'Process of Anger' and the impact of poor thinking skills upon negative behaviours. Explain how, in response to a threatening trigger, the adrenal gland releases an extra dose of the adrenaline hormone. As this adrenaline begins to build up, physiological changes occur within the body – such as tensed muscles, increased heart rate etc.

It should be explained that if a rational cognitive response to these physiological changes does not occur, then an incident may happen involving verbal or physical abuse.

Once the situation is no longer of threat, adrenaline levels begin to return to normality, and the body begins to recover from the experience. Physiological responses after a physically or verbally abusive incident can result in tiredness, exhaustion, breathlessness, headaches, dizziness etc, as blood levels begin to return to their normal state.

Students should also understand that anger is a natural emotion, felt by all, and can be used to positively address upset and prompt motivation for change. Anger comes in many forms from mild annoyance, to irritation to intense fury.

Similarly, adrenaline is a natural hormone secreted in appropriate doses from the adrenal glands. Adrenaline is felt in response to excitement or fear, such as the physiological feelings of preparing for a frightening fairground ride, the thrill and buzz of watching a favourite team score a goal, the enjoyment of celebration etc.

Adrenaline hormones are also released from the adrenal glands when there is a threat of offence or attack. The Flight or Fight response can cause large amounts of adrenaline to be released due to the perceived threat, requiring a quick physiological decision to be made. This physiological response to

the perceived threatening situation will be exasperated by distorted and irrational thinking due to the rapid response needed to the situation.

Students should study the cycle of anger and identify the earliest contributing factor. Although the earliest triggers may be the fault and responsibility of the aggressor, it should be understood that unlike animals, humans should take responsibility for their own responses to conflict due to the sophisticated and rationalised way we are wired and skilled to think and make rational decisions, as opposed to animalistic and aggressive thinking and behaviour.

A very strong contributing factor towards the cycle of anger is the cognitive process of the individual mind. Positive, assertive thinking skills can allow young people to identify warning signs of conflict, and prepare safe exit strategies, which would ultimately prevent an escalation of conflict and violence.

Explore the physiological responses to anger, but ensure students understand that anger is the physical result of other underlying feelings, and it is important to make the separate distinctions in order to address and tackle the primary triggers for the feeling of anger.

Some physiological responses to anger are;

Increased breathing
Dry mouth
Increased heart rate
Increased blood pressure
Flushed face
Dilated pupils
Nausea
Tense muscles
Head/Stomach ache
Hotness
Shaking
Numbness
Increased adrenaline flow
Shaking/Trembling
Sweaty hands / body parts

Some of the underlying causes of anger are when one feels;

Injustice has been experienced
Insulted or unjustly criticised
Frustrated or agitated
Loss of control

Now students should be able to identify, from a personal perspective, the types of physical responses they experience when faced with a situation which arouses angry feelings or thoughts. Students should also be able to self identify some of the underlying triggers to their own anger.

Discuss the concept of 'Personal space' and encourage the students to consider when this 'space' becomes invaded or threatened. It should also be discussed if it would ever be considered too late, once this space is threatened, to prevent the use of violence by either party, as young people can often lack assertive skills once embroiled in conflict. As the situation spirals out of control, so does the irrational behavioural responses of young people.

Students should be encouraged to consider ways in which this conflict may be avoided, such as not retaliating to the point where either person's 'personal space' becomes threatened and defended. The key point here is for students to begin to understand the need to identify warning signs of possible conflict as early as possible, which would allow adequate time for positive and rational decision making.

Once students have demonstrated an understanding of the physiological process of anger, they should be introduced to the psychological process, which accompanies angry internal feelings. Some negative, defensive thoughts in response to a perceived threat may be;

It's them or me!
He/She/They deserve it!
He/She/They disrespected me!
He/She/They need telling!
He/She/They need showing!
I'll get Him/Her/Them back!

Referring back to the 'process of Anger', ask students to consider if these negative, defensive thoughts would help the physiological response to

conflict to become more intense and severe and push the conflict into crisis stage where violence would probably occur.

Explain that the thoughts outlined are negative and will therefore ultimately influence actions and behaviours to also be negative. Introduce the Cognitive Behavioural Therapy (C.B.T) concept that demonstrates how our actions and behaviours are primarily shaped by our own thought (cognition) processes.

TRIGGER➞THOUGHT➞FEELING➞BEHAVIOUR

Present this theory using as many analogies and examples as possible to illustrate the overall concept that;

Positive thinking = Positive behaviour

and

Negative thinking = Negative behaviour.

Refer back to the negative thoughts already highlighted in relation to conflict, and demonstrate how different, positive, alternative, assertive thoughts would predict different responses that would ultimately prevent the use of violence.

Students should be encouraged to understand that as young people, they have a legal right to be 'protected' from harm or threat of harm. Therefore, the whole myth of the 'no grass' mentality should be explored for young people to understand how their existence as young adolescents makes them vulnerable members of society.

Young people should therefore feel it is their common right to inform appropriate adults of the issues they face, especially in relation to the threat of harm. Young people are legally entitled to the help and support of parents, police, teachers etc in managing conflict, rather than take the situation into their own hands, and living and dealing with this threat of harm alone.

Workshop suggestion

Hand out some set scenarios, or have the student's create some brief fictional details about a situation of conflict and anger involving young

PAL

people. Weapon or violence related newspaper stories may also be used as a basis for this exercise.

These scenarios/stories should then be unravelled to show the possible thought processes of the characters involved in the conflict. Both aspects should be depicted – negative and positive thoughts and behaviours.

Students should demonstrate an understanding of assertive approaches, by considering the early warning signs and promoting de-escalation through positive, alternative thinking patterns.

Students could create a 2 short film 'scenes', resulting in both a positive and a negative ending.

TRIGGER

THOUGHT

FEELING

ACTION

Staying Safe

Students should be reminded that maintenance of one's personal space and an adoption of exit strategies used from an early point in a situation of conflict is key to personal safety.

Refer back to any Conflict and Anger Management work already covered to re-iterate the importance of spotting warning signs of escalation as early as possible, to allow for the safe exiting out of a possibly dangerous situation.

Although assertive self-management of conflict is an ultimate key to prevention of weapon related revenge and reprisal, it is also as equally important for students to consider and adopt external safety strategies.

Some 'Staying Safe' ideas are suggested below.

Body Language - Try to promote assertive, but not aggressive body language, by walking like you know where you are heading. Do not 'swagger' up the street like you are looking for trouble, even if you are feeling angry. Remember that eye contact is the first trigger to conflict. If you spot someone who you are trying to avoid, then literally avoid eye contact; this may put them off having a verbal exchange with you, as nobody wants to look like they are talking to themselves! Do not attempt to have a 'stare out'; this will only cause further confrontation. Facial expression can also indicate warning signs. Yours or someone else's angry facial expressions displayed during conflict may give a warning

PAL

that the situation is escalating and it is time to adopt an exit strategy out of the situation.

Tone of Voice - Try to remain calm and collective when verbally exchanging in a situation of conflict. Screaming and shouting, or making threats will only cause your opponent to strike back at you. If the situation is verbally escalating out of control, do not retaliate, stay calm and leave.

Recognise the signs - Keep check of your own internal warning signs that you are becoming angry. Also keep check on other people's actions. If they begin to show external signs of physical anger then it is probably time to leave.

Don't attract attention - Keep your personal belongings such as mobile phones and music players discrete. These items may cause for attention to be drawn to you and make you a possible target for attack from others seeking financial or material gain from crime.

Stick with trustworthy friends - Keep check of who your 'real' friends are. Steer clear of any 'mad' friends who may cause conflict with other people. Be aware of any friends who pose anger management problems and spot the signs of dangerous or reckless behaviour in good time to allow for a safe exit. Stay with friends when out socialising and always attempt to go home in a manner which is safe for all.

Avoid 'gangs' - Steer around any big groups who may be about to cross your path. If needed, subtly cross over and again, avoid eye contact. A gang of unruly youths may be spoiling for a fight but if you are a safe distance from them you will probably feel a lot less threatened.

Out and About - On buses, although you may feel it is 'uncool', it is safer to sit downstairs rather than at the top. Similarly, on single Decker transport, it is probably safer to sit within the middle/front area. Unruly, delinquent youths will normally congregate at the top and back of public transport, usually to hide their unlawful behaviour, such as smoking. On trains, it is safer to sit in an occupied, rather than

empty carriage. Other passengers may put off any would-be attackers, as they would witness the conflict. Stay alert at all times, making sure that you are keeping an eye on your surroundings instead of listening to music and daydreaming. Stick to well lit streets and areas, avoiding dark alleyways and shortcuts.

Talk to an adult - Remember, you are a young person, and therefore should not have to carry the burden of threat on your shoulders. Inform an appropriate adult of any issues you are facing or experiencing. An adult will normally handle a situation more rationally than a young person would. If you are frightened of any revenge or reprisal, speak to an anonymous confidential service to gain help, advice and support.

Some tips for young people to remember if they ever face the threat of a weapon being used against them;

DO walk away **immediately** if somebody who is holding a knife or any other weapon confronts you

DO walk away **immediately** if you are confronted by somebody whom you have a great suspicion is carrying a knife or any other weapon

DO NOT try to take the knife from the attacker, it will cause injury or cause a scuffle in which someone is bound to be seriously physically hurt

DO NOT try to persuade or negotiate any kind of reason with the potential attacker, instead walk away **immediately**

DO NOT retaliate by carrying a weapon of your own in case of any further threat of attack

DO tell a responsible adult

DO inform the police

Dependent upon time and resources, introduce some basic First Aid to the students. Students should consider the vital part they could play in saving a life if they were to be with, or find, someone physically injured.

Spotting the Signs

Indications of weapon carrying, and in particular Gang membership, may be identified by the following signs;

Students displaying gang Graffiti or symbols upon their personal or school property

Student's found to be in possession of drugs, weapons or large, unexplained amounts of cash

Regular groupings of youths within isolated sets and showing hostility towards other groups of young people

The claiming of certain areas as 'territory'

Adoption of 'codes of dress'

Rapid, drastic falls in attainment and achievement coupled with sudden visibility of expensive clothing, jewellery or material items not attributable to personal wealth

Assessment

It is often a difficult task to assess and evidence learning, when teaching is primarily concerned with the development of the affective learning domain. However, it is hoped that the various suggested activities throughout this resource will allow for the cognitive and psychomotor learning domains to also become stimulated for students, thus promoting holistic learning. Differentiation techniques should be incorporated into objectives to ensure effective learning for all.

In relation to this resource, teaching which falls within the affective learning domain strives for students to adopt alternative ways of thinking, to allow them to make positive and informed decisions related to weapon crime. Below is an example of some questions, which may provide a checklist evidence base for observational assessments of attitudinal discussion and debate tasks completed by students;

	Y	N
1. The Student co-operated well		
2. The Student listened well to others		
3. The student challenged others calmly and assertively		
4. The Student contributed ideas		
5. The Student supported peers and was patient		
6. The Student contributed well towards problem solving		
7. The Student was a leader of the group		
8. The Student was a passive group member		
9. The Student made positive contribution towards written / IT tasks		
10.The Student gave constructive feedback		

PAL

Knife or Life

(Some creative activities)

(1)   Peer group agreement

The overall aim of this educative process has been to raise practitioners, as well as students, awareness levels in understanding the complex area of weapon carrying and gang membership.

This awareness should hopefully lead to a collective agreement between the students, that conflict should be managed in a way not involving the threat or use of a weapon.

Ask students, if they would consider carrying a weapon if they knew 100% that their enemy was not. Commonly, students will respond with *'well, how do I know they have/haven't, it's not worth taking the chance'*.

Explain to students that the 'Power' is currently in their hands, to make their peer group environment a safe place. Encourage the students to agree to NEVER resort to the threat of weapon use against someone as a response to conflict and anger.

Students who refuse to agree to this sanction should be persuaded to understand and envisage the long-term benefits of such an approach.

Students must also consider the chance of a weapon being turned against

PAL

them during a fight, rather than being turned on the target of attack by them. Therefore, a weapon will often fail to 'defend' the carrier, but instead possibly cut their life short.

Students, who are still undecided as to whether to agree to forbid the carrying of weapons within their peer group, may be presented with a FOR and AGAINST carrying weapons argument, by their fellow peers. This may offer an alternative route to persuasion.

If students eventually all agree, have them create and sign a 'Contract', possibly onto Flipchart paper. Again, artwork and graphic skills could be used to adopt and incorporate an anti weapon-carrying slogan onto the display.

This signed agreement could be displayed within a common meeting area of the students, to remind them of the important peer decision making process travelled through, to draw up a positive peer attitude towards the prevention of weapon related crime.

(2) Discussion Points/Cards

Use the suggested topics below to generate group/ individual discussion and debate. This open peer dialogue may provide a realistic assessment of the groups understanding, interpretation and perceptions of weapon related crime.

> You can get shot by the police for carrying/threatening to use a replica gun to harm someone?

> The consequences of weapon crime affect the whole community?

> Communities are now unsafe and overrun with delinquent youths?

> It is a parental responsibility to address weapon carrying by their young?

> Rap music is to blame for young people's attitude towards weapon crime and gang membership?

British gangs are influenced by American gangs?

Knives are less dangerous than guns?

Knives are just as dangerous as guns?

The sentence for carrying a knife should be the same as for carrying a gun?

Is it easy for a young person to get hold of a gun?

Is it easy for a young person to get hold of a knife?

Weapon crime exists only because of drug selling?

Most young people involved with carrying knives end up as knife victims?

Only men use weapons?

Girls do not use weapons?

Weapons are a fashion accessory amongst young people?

You feel safe if you are carrying a weapon?

Weapons for self defence are okay?

Teachers should search more young people for weapons?

Metal detectors should be placed in all schools?

Using a weapon solves a dispute?

Carrying a weapon can make you feared?

People who use weapons do not care about physical consequences?

Police should be armed at all times?

Police should stop and search all young people who hang on the streets?

Weapon crime is only a problem in big urban cities?

A replica gun looks identical to a real gun?

It is right for the criminal consequences for carrying or threatening to use a replica gun are the same as that for guns?

Gang members will most likely become victims of weapon attacks?

Street / Youth Gangs distribute most drugs?

Most gangs operate criminal activities?

Gangs are always male?

Britain has a youth 'gang' problem?

Media, TV, Music, Games Newspapers, all hype up gang and weapon use?

Violent films/media can influence gang members to inflict violence?

You can never exit once you have joined a gang?

Dysfunctional and disjointed family networks are most responsible for causing young people to join gangs?

(3)   Artwork

Anti weapon carrying messages promoted on visual posters and T-Shirts may promote a positive attitude and awareness of weapon crime. Brainstorming and Mind mapping exercises, presented pictorially, would also promote an artistic approach towards raising awareness levels of students.

(4)   If I ruled the World for One day!

Students could consider what their political strategy would be if they 'Ruled the World' for 1 day.

The concept behind this exercise is for the students to promote a zero tolerance culture towards weapon carrying, thus creating a safe and stable world for the future generations.

Young people could work in teams to produce a Parliamentary Bill, outlining a governmental approach to tackle weapon use of gang involvement amongst young people. Some suggestions that would enhance and strengthen current preventative strategies could be;

Laws – tougher sentences?

Metal Detection – more visible in more public places?

Stop and Search – more people?

Body Scans – in all public places?

Search Powers – extended to Community representatives?

Knife Amnesties – more often?

Programmes for Offenders – make more accessible to the whole of the young person population?

Encourage the students to think of new, imaginative measures which could ultimately stamp out weapon related crime, such as;

More Community Policing

More young friendly community resources

Harsher consequences for young people

Total ban on any kind of Rifle or Air Gun to prevent mixed messages being given to young people

Total ban on the carrying of ANY bladed article, no matter the blade size

Tackle social exclusion

Provide safe exit routes for Gang members

Intensive police surveillance of drug dealing to break down gang existence

Free Drop-In centres providing safe, preventative help

Encourage anonymous information from the community

Preventative education from as early as 5 years of age and throughout adolescence

(5)   M'Lord

Present the students with a fictional Court Case – containing brief details about a weapon related crime, the offender's background and history, the victim's background and history, and a description of the overall event and the negative impact that occurred. Random media stories may be used to provide details for the case.

Alternatively, use a relative headline from a Newspaper. A choice of fatal stories within the public domain is given below. These stories are particularly upsetting as they all have a fatal ending, but are true crimes and therefore offer a realistic perspective.

(1) Victim - Joe Dinsdale (m), 17, 11 February 2008, Hull, East Yorkshire.

'A father's heartbreak as violent Britain claims another victim'[8]

Dinsdale died in hospital from a stab wound to the stomach after being attacked after an argument. A male aged 21 years, was found guilty of murder and ordered to serve a minimum of fifteen-and-a-half years, as well as thirty months concurrently for each of five counts of supplying a Class A drug. [9]

(2) Victim - Joshua Mitchell (m), 17, 22 March 2008, South Kessock, Inverness, Invernesshire.

'A Teenager murdered a boy with learning difficulties after stabbing him once through the heart in a brutal unprovoked attack'[10]

Mitchell was stabbed near his parents' home in an unprovoked attack by a 17-year-old male, who had been drinking and taking Valium pills and was carrying a knife. He admitted the murder and was sentenced to serve at least thirteen years in jail. [11]

---

8   Written for The Mail
9   Institute of Race Relations
10   Written for The Herald
11   Institute of Race Relations

(3) Victim - Ashley Horton (m), 16, 27 March 2008, Kings Norton, Birmingham, Midlands.

'A 16-year-old Birmingham boy was stabbed to death after a row over a £10 note, a neighbour said today'[12]

Horton died in hospital after being stabbed in the leg at a boarded-up house. His attacker had been a habitual knife carrier and was convicted of his murder. [13]

(4)   Victim - Robert Spence (m), 17, 02 May 2008, Reading, Berkshire.

'Boy killed in street fight named' [14]

Spence, also known as Junior, was stabbed at the end of a night out in Reading town centre. He and his group of friends became involved in an altercation with another group, unknown to them at the time, who had driven to Reading from Bristol for a night out and who then armed themselves with knives and samurai swords to enact a revenge attack after the earlier altercation. Three men were convicted of murder and attempted murder and sentenced to minimum terms of between twenty and twenty-two years each. [15]

---

12   Written for the Birmingham Post
13   Institute of Race Relations
14   Written for BBC News Online
15   Institute of Race Relations

(5) Victim - Frazer Endicott (m), 19, 7 June 2008, Balby, Doncaster, South Yorkshire.

'Devoted 23-year-old father stabbed to death on a nightclub dance floor'[16]

Endicott died after being found stabbed on a pavement in the early hours. His half-brother aged 25 years, in a row over beer after the pair had been drinking, killed him. This attacker was sentenced to life for murder and will serve a minimum of fifteen years.[17]

(6) Victim - Conor Black (m), 16, 16 August 2008, Harpurhey, Manchester, Greater Manchester.

'Stab Death; Boy, 16 held' [18]

Black died after being stabbed in the shoulder in the early hours after attending a house party. He was murdered after an argument over an Xbox games console. Black was smashed over the head with a can of lager, before being stabbed in the back as he turned to escape. His attacker, aged 16, boasted about the killing afterwards and went onto to admit manslaughter but was found guilty of murder and sentenced to serve a minimum of eleven years. [19]

---

16   Written for The Mail
17   Institute of Race Relations
18   Written for The Manchester Evening News
19   Institute of Race Relations

(7)Victim - Luke Howard (m), 16, 30 August 2008, Knotty Ash, Liverpool, Merseyside.

'Teen stabbed to death after party row'[20]

Howard was stabbed twelve times during an argument at a party, after a group of teenage boys drank alcohol, smoked cannabis and snorted cocaine. Howard was apparently 'prodding' a 15 year old attending the 'party'. They had been deliberately 'winding each other up'. This escalated into a full-blown fight between them both. Howard was pinning the other teenager down on a bed and stabbing at his face with the screwdriver. Howard's attacker then reached for something to defend himself with but ended up grabbing a knife, which had been brought into the room to open wine with. The judge and jury accepted Howard's attacker's claim of self-defence. He denied murder but admitted manslaughter and was initially sentenced to seven years' detention, reduced to four-and-a-half years after appeal on the grounds of provocation and his age at the time of the attack.[21]

---

20 Written for The Liverpool Echo
21 Institute of Race Relations

(8) Victim - Courtney Eaton (m), 17, 5 September 2008, Winton, Salford, Greater Manchester.

'Teenager stabbed in 'street' row' [22]

Eaton died of stab wounds after a fight near a petrol station. A male, 18, had been drinking heavily and carried a fold-up knife, for protection, he said. Eaton's friend had shouted an insult at the male's brother - a 'minor incident', as the police described it. The teenage attacker was found guilty of manslaughter after insisting he did not mean to use the weapon. He was sentenced to eight years' detention in a young offenders' institution. The attacker also admitted carrying the knife for self-protection and pleaded guilty to carrying an offensive weapon - he will serve three years for this offence concurrently. [23]

(9) Victim - Dale Robertson (m), 18, 7 September 2008, Parsons Cross, Sheffield, South Yorkshire.

'Teenager knifed to death in postcode gang battle' [24]

Robertson died after being stabbed following a party, after a row over an Xbox games console. The Times (8 September 2008) reported: 'A teenager was stabbed to death when rival "postcode" gangs, some armed with baseball bats and knives, fought running battles in the street after clashing at a girl's 16th birthday party. Up to 40 youths were involved in the fight in

Sheffield'. Two teenagers were convicted of murder. They will serve ten and eleven and a-half years minimum. [25]

---

22   Written for BBC News Online
23   Institute of Race Relations
24   Written for The Mail
25   Institute of Race Relations

PAL

(10) Victim - Joseph Lappin (m), 16, 20 October 2008,Everton, Liverpool, Merseyside.

'Boy, 16, stabbed to death outside youth club'[26]

Lappin died after being stabbed outside a youth club. He was murdered on 20 October after being chased by a gang. He had enjoyed a night with friends at the Shrewsbury House Youth Club in Everton. It was the first time he attended the church building and was there to support a friend's band. He and a friend were waiting for a lift home when they were

confronted and chased back to the youth club where they sought safety. But Lappin, a member of the Liverpool Scottish Regiment, received a fatal stab wound and his friend was knifed twice. Ten people were charged with Lappin's murder. [27]

(11) Victim - Kadeem Blackwood (m), 15, 11 November 2008, Derby, Derbyshire.

'Boy, 15, shot dead in gangland style attack'[28]

The 15-year-old was shot in the chest. A fight had been arranged with some members of rival gang A1. Blackwood was carrying a knife and was then shot himself in Caxton Street recreation ground in Sunnyhill, Derby. He was taken to hospital where he died from his injuries. Three teenage males were found guilty of his murder and sentenced to twenty-three and twenty-one years respectively. [29]

---

26   Written for The Telegraph
27   Institute of Race Relations
28   Written for The Telegraph
29   Institute of Race Relations

(12) Victim - Faridon Alizada (m), 18, 5 January 2008, Erith, Bexley, Southeast London.

'Stabbed 3 times in chest latest victim was 'caught up in drugs fued' [30]

Alizada and two other 16-year-old teenagers were attacked by a 32-year-old man, who was found guilty of murder and sentenced to a minimum twenty-five years for the murder and twenty-two years for two counts of wounding with intent, to run concurrently. The killer, a cocaine addict, burst into their flat, stabbing Alizada and the two other teenagers who used the room to take crack and sell drugs. The killer was a regular customer of the teenagers who, it was alleged by the Evening Standard and the London Paper, were associated with either the Woolwich Boys gang or the IVS (InVincible Soldiers) Gang. The killer had already tried to rob the flat the previous week and had been to the flat three or four times that day and returned with a friend having failed to get drugs from another dealer and with the intention of robbing the boys. The killer, a former professional bare-knuckle fighter, had a string of violent offences dating back to 1992. [31]

---

30   Written for the London Evening Standard
31   Institute of Race Relations

(13) Victim - Lyle Tulloch (m), 15, 3 May 2008, Elephant & Castle, Southwark, South London.

'Teenager, 15, knifed to death in flats stairwell'[32]

> *Tulloch was stabbed thirteen times in a stairwell after being accused of stealing 18-year-old's mobile phone at a party. Two teenagers were found guilty of murder and sentenced to a minimum of twelve years each.* [33]

(14) Victim - Jimmy Mizen (m), 16, 10 May 2008, Lewisham, Southeast London.

'Teen killed by shard of glass from shop window' [34]

> *Mizen was killed when his attacker, aged 19, flung glass at his face in a bakery, leaving him bleeding to death. His attacker was found guilty of murder and sentenced to a minimum of fourteen years.* [35]

---

32   Written for The Guardian
33   Institute of Race Relations
34   Written for The Independent
35   Institute of Race Relations

(15) Victim - Rob Knox (m), 18, 24 May 2008, Sidcup, Bexley, Southeast London.

'Harry Potter actor stabbed to death in mobile phone vendetta'[36]

Knox was killed after being stabbed five times outside a nightclub in Sidcup, southeast London. The attacker was found guilty of murder and sentenced to serve a minimum of twenty years and concurrent sentences for wounding. [37]

(16) Victim - Ben Kinsella (m), 16, 29 June 2008, Islington, north London.

'How a misplaced glance led to innocent teen's murder' [38]

Kinsella was chased down an Islington street by three teenagers and stabbed eleven times. The attack came after a series of earlier fights between gangs of youths and had started when one of the attackers, aged 19, felt a group not linked to Kinsella had disrespected him. This attacker and a friend then confronted a friend of Kinsella's. Shortly after this, the attacker and his friend were attacked by about thirty youths. This attacker's friend had a cut to his head that required treatment. This attacker then left the pub, but phoned two teenage friends, returned to the pub, and chased Kinsella's group who were stood outside, before kicking Kinsella to the ground and stabbing him. The three were convicted of murder and sentenced to minimum of nineteen-year terms[39]

---

36   Written for The Sunday Times
37   Institute of Race Relations
38   Written for The Telegraph
39   Institute of Race Relations

PAL

(17) Victim - Charles Junior Hendricks (m), 18, 24 August 2008, Walthamstow, Waltham Forest northeast London.

'Boy, 17, arrested over murder of 18 year old found stabbed to death in London' [40]

Hendricks was found with stab wounds as two or three males were seen running away. He died shortly afterwards. The Press described him as being caught up in a gang dispute. Although some teenagers have been charged with his murder, no one has yet been brought to trial. [41]

(18) Victim - Shaquille Smith (m), 14, 31 August 2008, of Hackney, northeast London.

'Gang jailed for murder of innocent teenager' [42]

Smith was caught in the middle of a dispute between two gangs – one from the London Fields area and one from the E9 postcode. It is believed up to fifteen youths from the Fields Boys were involved. Six teenagers, all members of the London Fields gang, were convicted of Smith's murder and jailed for minimum terms of between fifteen and eighteen years. [43]

N.B. All of the above examples of knife related incidents have been taken from a report commissioned by the Institute of Race Relations - Youth Deaths: The reality behind the Knife Crime Debate, Briefing Paper no.5, written by Rebecca Wood and also from the mentioned media source.

---

40   Written for The Telegraph
41   Institute of Race Relations
42   Written for the Times
43   Institute of Race Relations

After being introduced to this exercise and given a chosen case, students should assign themselves roles; Solicitor, Judge, Offender, Victim, Parents/Family members, Youth Offending Service (YOS)/Probation Officer. The remaining students should play the Jury members.

Each character should then present their case to the Judge, explaining any mitigation, fault, regret and hurt related to the incident/offence. The Judge listen to the summing up of evidence, in order to make a fully informed decision of the consequence, having considered all of the factual information presented by the Jury on behalf of the characters.

The Judge and Jury members should make some written notes whilst listening to the evidence given by the characters. This will help when giving the 'Summary of Evidence' and an ultimate decision.

A discussion should then be held as one collective group with the students to assess the realism of the consequences proposed, considering motivation, offending history, criminal lifestyle and victim impact. Any difference in student opinions should be explored.

The headline stories described cover a diverse range of topics that can be used to assist any of the areas that are explored throughout this resource. It will help students to gain a realistic and true meaning of weapon related crime and the associated consequences if real stories are used as illustration and reference.

PAL

Sources and References

Aldridge J, Medina J, Sharp C., Delinquent Youth Groups and Offending Behaviour, Findings from the 2004 Offending, Crime and Justice Survey, Home Office Online report (2006)

Crime in England and Wales, Home Office statistical bulletin (2006/2007)

Decker S H, Winkle V, Life in gangs: family, friends and violence, Cambridge University Press (1996)

Klein M W, Street gangs and street workers, Prentice Hall, Englewood Cliffs, NT (1971)

Lemos and Crane, Fear and Fashion: the use of knives and other weapons by young people, The Bridge House Trust (2004)

Marshall B, Webb B, Tilley N, Rationalisation of current research on guns, gangs and other weapons: Jill Dando Institute of Crime Science University College, London (2005)

Mizen P, The changing state of youth, Palgrave Macmillan (2004)

Muncie J, Youth and crime, 2nd Edition, SAGE Publications (2004)

Pitts J, Safer Society, Macro Publications (2006)

Rutter M, Giller H, Hagell A, Anti Social behaviour by young people, Cambridge University Press

Youth Justice Board, Mori Youth Study, Ipsos Mori (2004)

Wood, R, Youth Deaths: The Reality behind the Knife Crime Debate, Briefing Paper No.5, Institute of Race Relations (2008)

PAL

Lightning Source UK Ltd.
Milton Keynes UK
UKOW05f1815110813

215206UK00001B/95/P